Bilingual Baby: Confessions of a Latina Woman

Karina Ortiz

BookLeaf Publishing

India | USA | UK

Presentation by *BookLeaf Publishing*

Web: www.bookleafpub.com

E-mail: info@bookleafpub.com

ISBN: 9789358318142

First edition 2023

ACKNOWLEDGEMENT

Thank you to my dear friends who took time to read these before I put them into a collection. You are truly Godsends and I couldn't have done it without your help and encouragement to keep moving forward.

Traveler

First-gen
college kid
obtains valuable knowledge.

Takes
the road
less traveled by,

pursues
her dream—
chases the stars—

until
she runs
out of breath.

Knowledge is power.
Run rabbit, run.

Papi

Factories
contain images
of my father—

Nuyorican,
Boricua, Taíno,
Proud Puerto Rican—

smooth
talker, negotiator—
bargains with everyone.

Workaholic,
helping hand,
nunca se descansa.

Calculates everyone's moves.
I'm intimidated too.

La madre mía

Go-getter
attitude. Immigrant
from Lima, *Perú.*

Mujer
de la
casa. A woman-of-all-trades:

Mother,
Wife, Cook,
all the above,

but
don't think
for one second

she is inarticulate—
la chancla volará.

Paterson

I'm
a trespasser
in my childhood—

home
no longer
found in *bodegas*,

East
18th Street
or Glen Rock —

is it even
called that
anymore?

Home: bittersweet recollections.
Paterson: ghostly obsession.

But We Were Happy

Jonathan and I lived in Paterson where
our futures were bleak, but
we were happy in the presence of each other.

We lived with
our mother who we rarely saw because
we knew she worked countless jobs.
Our sister, Jeanette, who was 13, babysat us but
we knew she was too much of a baby herself.
Our brother Raul, who was 15,
we knew was busy having a baby himself.
Our father was rarely present as he spent
countless days,
we would come to find, held captive to cocaine
and alcohol.
Regardless, our happiness prevailed.
We were fortunate to have each other in the
chaos of
our family that never had time for our love.

Lake Days

*Poner
ropas de
baño para nadar.*

Papi
fills the
cooler with ice,

grabs
Puerto Rican
pan para sandwiches.

Jonathan
and I
fight — "Mom's side."

He
wins, I
lose — like always.

Hiss
at him
with my "claws."

When we arrive,
Lake cleanses all.

Pine Island Weekends

Removed—
away from
the bustling city,

travel
Upstate to
see certain family.

Spend
hours with
our cousin Jovanny.

Live
life blissfully
in Pine Island.

Quisiera volver al
tiempo — disfrutarlo más.

Corn State

Everyday
shocked by
friendly, neighborly Iowans.

Curious
about how
such hospitality exists.

Always
perplexed by
the insane idioms –

What
does "Having
a cow" mean?

New home: Iowa.
Confused corn girl.

Mac and Cheese

High
school sweethearts
since age 17

wandered
prairie fields
filled with green,

walked
fur babies
through wild serene,

built
a home
as flourishing teens —

sometimes I dwell
on innocent memories.

More Than Disease

If you ask me what my sister is like,
I can list 1,000 personality traits:
The sunshine in the room,
The iron fist of doom,
The silver lining
That combats gloom—
Those are merely a few.

If you ask me what my sister is like,
I can list 1,000 warnings from a mother:
Matti stop letting Steel out of his cage,
Ava do NOT forget to comb your hair again,
Matti and Ava stop fighting or Dance Party is
over—
That's a snippet of her life.

If you ask me what my sister is like,
I can list 1,000 ways she's the best sister ever:
Kari, you need to put him in his place.
Jonathan hasn't messaged lately; I hope he's
okay.
Do you think I overstepped with him?—
The daily worries that cross her mind.

If you ask me what my sister is like,
I can list 1,000 ways she's a dependable wife:
Babe, I packed your lunch with fresh veggies.
Babe, I worked on our budget plan, it's right
here.
Babe, use my car for right now; we'll figure it
out—
A manager of the household.

And if you ask me what my sister is like,
I would say she is a mother, sister, and wife
but **not once** would I list the way Lupus
tries to dominate every single day of her life.

Stepmom

"I've
been Gay
all my life,"

words
my papi
will never forget.

Humor
melted his
wary, vigilant heart—

created
an elixir
from the start—

thank you, Gay,
for giving
him

life of laughter
and love thereafter.

Deep Dive

Rays from the sun scatter across the ocean,
Highlighting the waves' blue-green motion.

Reflections of light glimmer with belief,
Making the surface of the water beam.

I wonder what lies beneath,
The serene surface of the scene.

I place troubles on the waves as they gently meet
the shore,
As they carry them away to the deep ocean floor.

Oceans hide sorrows in profound deep,
To be buried away and put to sleep.

For a moment, all is calm and filled with peace,
The heaviness has passed; been released.

Yet there's a sinister feeling lingering above,
In which I can't quite get ahold of—

I struggle to breathe in spite of air—
I clutch at my throat with shock, a scare.

Then I remembered how the sun went down,
And cast a weighted darkness all around

While I walked into the deep profound
To return to my sorrows; I chose to

D
   R
      O
         W
            N.

Tus lunares

- Dedicado a D

Tus lunares me miran,
vuelvo a mirarlos.
Arte en la forma
de dos círculos oscuros
quedan enraizados en mi mente.
Los veo en mis sueños,
esos dos lunares—
casi se conectan a tus labios—
Dos pedazos de ti
que quiero sentir
sobre mí.

Radiant

Tender kisses
like light rain
pattering drops of fire
causing high flames.

Our hearts connect from
enduring alike pain,
as they loudly drum
from their domain.

I stare at your eyes
beautiful and bright
casting a glow like
the Northern Lights.

Our palms collide
dampened with sweat —
our love will be one
of no regret.

Ode to the Wasp

All this space but choose to fly near my face,
I grow tired of the constant buzzing.
I hope you learn to discern your airspace—
Perchance mistake me constantly bluffing,

I assure you—I truly wish I were,
But these yellow and black beasts of nature
Are causes to produce murderous slur.
They manage to find me— without failure,

Though there many flowers in the garden—
They repeatedly seek out my presence.
I cannot fathom giving such pardon
Upon pests who are wholly unpleasant.

All this space, while I am seen a headcase
Simply because they deem me a workplace.

Rainstorm

Grey
skies loom
on the horizon.

Exhilaration
rushes through
my awaiting spirit.

There's
a twinkle
in my eyes,

as the lightning
strikes open
fields.

Rain produces hope,
as Heaven strobes.

Cycles

Ruby
razors wave
to old bones.

Shadows
whisper pain —
your skin moans.

The Devil comes
knocking, wrecking
down

your barricaded door.
You succumb —
mutilated.

You versus you,
an endless war.

Maldición generacional

Do not express
emotions here
mija.

If you do,
no te
ayudaré.

En vez, te
dejare sufrir
sola.

No lloramos aquí —
luchamos para
sobrevivir.

Pero no siento
humano sin sentir.

Bebé bilingüe

Ser
bilingüe es
una gran bendición —

I
can switch
back and forth

whenever
I wish —
como ahorita mismo.

También, es difícil
ser bilingüe —
tratan

de sofocar la
voz del futuro.

9 789358 318142